Christine Ngan

Employment Contracts in the Banking Industry

Christine Ngari

Employment Contracts in the Banking Industry

Short-term contracting

LAP LAMBERT Academic Publishing

Impressum / Imprint

Bibliografische Information der Deutschen Nationalbibliothek: Die Deutsche Nationalbibliothek verzeichnet diese Publikation in der Deutschen Nationalbibliografie; detaillierte bibliografische Daten sind im Internet über http://dnb.d-nb.de abrufbar.

Alle in diesem Buch genannten Marken und Produktnamen unterliegen warenzeichen-, marken- oder patentrechtlichem Schutz bzw. sind Warenzeichen oder eingetragene Warenzeichen der jeweiligen Inhaber. Die Wiedergabe von Marken, Produktnamen, Gebrauchsnamen, Handelsnamen, Warenbezeichnungen u.s.w. in diesem Werk berechtigt auch ohne besondere Kennzeichnung nicht zu der Annahme, dass solche Namen im Sinne der Warenzeichen- und Markenschutzgesetzgebung als frei zu betrachten wären und daher von jedermann benutzt werden dürften.

Bibliographic information published by the Deutsche Nationalbibliothek: The Deutsche Nationalbibliothek lists this publication in the Deutsche Nationalbibliografie; detailed bibliographic data are available in the Internet at http://dnb.d-nb.de.

Any brand names and product names mentioned in this book are subject to trademark, brand or patent protection and are trademarks or registered trademarks of their respective holders. The use of brand names, product names, common names, trade names, product descriptions etc. even without a particular marking in this works is in no way to be construed to mean that such names may be regarded as unrestricted in respect of trademark and brand protection legislation and could thus be used by anyone.

Coverbild / Cover image: www.ingimage.com

Verlag / Publisher:
LAP LAMBERT Academic Publishing
ist ein Imprint der / is a trademark of
AV Akademikerverlag GmbH & Co. KG
Heinrich-Böcking-Str. 6-8, 66121 Saarbrücken, Deutschland / Germany
Email: info@lap-publishing.com

Herstellung: siehe letzte Seite /
Printed at: see last page
ISBN: 978-3-8443-9702-4

TABLE OF CONTENTS

1. INTRODUCTION

1.1 Background of the Study

Houseman, (2001) defined short-term contracting as a contract which terminates on a specified date or on the occurrence of an event which is certain to occur on a particular date. Short-term contracts may be used to cover sickness; maternity leave where the date that the substantive post holder will return is not known; other period of paid/unpaid leave where the end date is not known; cover a temporary reduction in the hours of a member of staff; cover a short-term temporary increase in workload (Abowd et al, 1999).

Many countries have adopted two-tier reforms that, while increasing flexibility at the margin, left unchanged mandates applying to already existing contracts. As a result, new contractual arrangements governed by less stringent rules were introduced. Subsequently, some of these new forms of contract rapidly gained importance (Maurin, 2000). In Kenya, it was also the case that new forms of work also developed. This saw the introduction of fixed-term or temporary employment contracts which has increasingly gained momentum (Matindni, 2006). Rationalization of the growing share of these temporary work arrangements has been offered within an adjustment cost framework. In this context, firms hire contingent workers because they want to save on future dismissal costs. Notwithstanding, the focus on adjustment costs alone may be too narrow.

Recent studies (e.g. Hunt, 2000; Maurin, 2000) dispute the common view that short-term contracts actually offer firms increased flexibility due to restrictions that typically apply to the rolling over of these contracts. Besides, there are a number of reasons other than saving on prospective firing costs that may make firms willing to use fixed-term contracts:

First, temporary workers may be preferred because they may be less costly to employ. Second, temporary contractual types, are preferred alternatives when temporary or temporarily vacant positions are being filled. Third, if there is uncertainty about the value of the match, fixed-term contracts may serve as screening devices. When the information about the true value of the match arrives, the match will be classified as good or bad depending on how its true value compares to the firm's reservation value. Accordingly, the match is either maintained or terminated. If match destruction is optimal the firing cost will be borne. Hence, in contexts like this, firms may find it optimal to hire workers on temporary contracts for a trial period and at a latter stage either offers them a permanent contract or dismiss them. Fourth, independently of any of the reasons above, using fixed-term contracts to all permanent positions may be part of the firm's personnel policy.

In the current world labor market, temporary forms of work, which include part-time work, temporary agency employment, independent contracts, and short-term hiring, are mostly used to accommodate workload fluctuations and to fill temporarily vacant positions, although, some employers report using flexible forms of employment to screen workers for regular positions (Autor, 2001, Houseman, 2001).

In the Kenyan labour market today, more and more people are employed in temporary jobs, including workers hired for short-term assignments through temporary help agencies, and workers hired directly by firms on short-term contracts. Banks have particularly reduced the number of permanent employees and increased the use of short-term workers.

These short term contracting workers are largely made up of local hires who possess certain skills and talents that are needed in several different areas of operations; and provide services that are just as important as those provided by permanent employees. However, the short-term workers receive no special benefits such as those received by their permanent contract counterparts. Yet, largely, these are local hires who are employed to perform similar services which require, at times, that they take time off of work for personal reasons. This study seeks to investigate the factors that have favoured increased use of the short-term contracts workers in the Kenyan banking industry.

1.1.1 The Banking Sector in Kenya

The Banking sector in Kenya is governed by the Companies Act, the Banking Act, the Central Bank of Kenya Act and the various prudential guidelines issued by the Central Bank of Kenya (CBK). The banking sector was liberalized in 1995 and exchange controls lifted. As at December 2008 there were forty six banking and non bank institutions, fifteen micro finance institutions and one hundred and nine foreign exchange bureaus. The banks have come together under the Kenya Bankers Association (KBA), which serves as a lobby for the banking sector's interests. The KBA serves as forum to address issues affecting members.

Over the last few years, the Banking sector in Kenya has continued to grow in assets, deposits, profitability and products offering. The growth has been mainly underpinned by: an industry wide branch network expansion strategy both in Kenya and in the East African community region; automation of a large number of services and a move towards emphasis on the complex customer needs rather than traditional 'off-the-shelf' banking products. Players in this sector have experienced increased competition over the last few years resulting from increased innovations among the players and new entrants into the market.

1.2 Statement of the Problem

In the last decade, there has been a sharp rise in the use of short-term contracts among corporate organizations in Kenya. As a break from the past, there has been a tendency among Kenyan banks to reduce the number of permanent employment contracts. In consequence, the banks have increasingly employed workers on short-term contracts. According to a study by Matindni, (2006) in 32 corporate firms, 9.2% of all employees were temporary. The study also found that 67% of the firms surveyed use temporary workers. However, it did not investigate why the firms use temporary employment contracts.

Short term contract employment is a practice in which organizations employ workers on temporary terms. The short-term contracts contain no incentives for initiation or continuation of employment that translates to job security. Many researchers (Guell and Petrongolo, 2003; Houseman, 2001; and Autor, 2001) seek to re-balance the debate on temporary employment which they consider to have been distorted by unfounded assertions. The view that short-term is of some advantage, to employers at least, is commonplace. For example, it is believed to increase labour market flexibility as well as widen the scope for employers to screen possible long-term recruits while they are temporarily employed. The larger question, however, is whether these advantages to employers should be allowed to outweigh the drawbacks on the side of employees. If all the drawbacks were suffered only by employers it might make sense to leave them to make up their own minds without regulation. However, despite efforts to minimize the disadvantages for workers, these are far from negligible. This study therefore, seeks to investigate the factors that favour the increased use of short term contracting option among the commercial banks in Kenya despite most of them recording huge profits.

4

1.3 General Objective

The overall objective of the study was to investigate the factors favouring the increased use of short-term contracting in the Kenyan banking sector.

1.4 Specific Objective

1. To investigate the cost implication of short-term contracts in the banking sector in Kenya.
2. To establish the extent to which workload fluctuation favours increased use of short-term contracts.
3. To assess how business uncertainty favours increased use of short-term contracts in the banking sector.
4. To investigate how employee screening practices favour increased use of short-term contracts in the banking sector.

1.5 Research Questions

1. What are the cost implications of short-term contracts in the banking sector.
2. To what extent do workload fluctuations favour short-term contracts in the banking sector?
3. How do business uncertainties favour increased use of short-term contracts in the banking sector?
4. How do employee-screening practices favour increased use of short-term contracts in the banking sector?

1.6 Significance of the Study

The findings of this study are expected to give an insight to various stakeholders of interest in this sector in different ways. These are as follows:-

1. The study will be useful to the banking industry as a whole and in particular those who practice this form of human resource procurement approach. The findings therefore is expected to furnish them with information that will be helpful to them in making rational decision regarding the short term contracting of human resources.

2. The finding may extend its tentacles of ideas beyond the sector and other industries or institutions practicing similar procurement approach as to the conditions which merit the use of short term contracting instead of perhaps employing the approach blindly without having any clear facts about this method of hiring.

3. To the labour market, the study will enable them understand why firms would be motivated to employ them on fixed-term contracts as opposed to permanent contracts.

4. To academicians and future researchers, this study is a stepping stone to deeper and more advance studies in the subject area. The results of the study will make a myriad of contributions to the literature on temporary employment practice. This will be part of scholarly articles useful to researchers who want to further the study; and to other wider stakeholders in the academic circles.

1.7 Limitations of the Study

Some of banks did not respond fully to some of the critical questions; hence this was anticipated to be one limitation to this study since most of information required for this study relied on their responses and incase data collected was insufficient, then generalization of the finding may not be representative of the actual scenario in the real corporate world. Secondly, inadequate financial resources actually hampered the researcher from obtaining all required information for the study, thus possibility of not having enough data to meet the objectives of the study.Thirdly,the extensive number of commercial banks and their locations made it quite time consuming for the researcher and her assistants.

1.8 Scope of the Study

The scope of the study as in terms of the area under investigation included cost implication, workload fluctuations, business uncertainty and employee screening. The study considered the banking institutions based in Nairobi Kenya since this is the capital city which is expected to host majority of educated and unemployed people who can be contracted by these banks on the terms under investigation. The study concentrated on aspects of cost implications, extent to which workload fluctuates business uncertainties and employee screening practices.

1.9 Definition of Terms

Adjustment costs

The expenses that a firm incurs when a change occurs in its workforce either by employees resigning, being fired or a new employee being hired

Employee screening

The process of evaluating an employee's ability to carry out the duties and responsibilities of a specific job

Freelance workers

Independent contractors that are usually hired by firms to perform specific tasks

Labour flexibility

The speed with which an organization can reorganize its workforce to adapt to fluctuations in business activity, this helps in achievement of equilibrium between the labour force demand and supply within the organization.

Short-term contract

A contract of employment for a definite period set in advance, usually less than year. A contract with a fixed start and end date is a fixed term or temporary contract even if it is likely to be renewed.

Variable

A variable is a measurable characteristic that assumes different values among the subjects. It is therefore, a logical way of expressing a particular attribute in a subject.

Data

Data refers to all the information a researcher gathers for the study.

CHAPTER TWO

2.0 LITERATURE REVIEW

2.1 Introduction

This chapter presents the past studies and literature on short-term contracts. It defines the concept, reviews the literature, and presents the critical review, the conceptual framework and a summary of the study.

2.2 Conceptual Framework

Conceptual framework is defined as the result of when a researcher conceptualizes the relationship between variables in the study and shows the relationship graphically or diagrammatically (Mugenda & Mugenda, 2003). The conceptual framework allows the quantitative conceptualization; operationalization, data collection and measurement of the variables identified (Neuman, 2000). According to Cooper & Schindler (2003) conceptual framework also presents the various variables in the study.

This study is based on the examination of the relationship between the dependent variable (increased short-term contracting) and the Independent variables (cost implication, workload fluctuation, business uncertainty and employee screening). The construct on which these two variables and its relationships are based are illustrated in figure 1 as follows:-

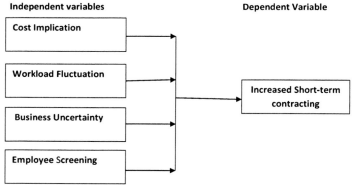

Figure 1: Conceptual Framework

2.2 .1 Short-term Contracting and Cost Implications

Autor, (2001) contends that firms employ short-term workers so as to avoid firing costs. According to Booth *et al* (2000), it is costly to discharge long-serving employees. Workers with sufficient length of service are entitled to statutory redundancy pay and can claim unfair dismissal. Insofar as these are simple transfers from the firm to the separating worker, there is no particular reason to avoid permanent appointments. A worker on a short-term contract will, in a competitive labour market, receive a higher wage that just offsets the loss of the expected value of redundancy pay. However, severance costs can contain a deadweight element.

Houseman, (2001) observe that there is a considerable cost in time and expense to a firm in being brought before an industrial tribunal to defend an unfair dismissal claim. For these reasons, firms might prefer to have a cushion of workers without employment rights who can be freely discharged in the event of adverse market conditions, even if the firm must pay a wage premium to these workers.

According to Booth et al (2000) there are a number of reasons why short-term workers may not in practice receive a compensating differential in the form of a higher wage than permanent workers. It is not efficient for workers in short-term contracts to invest heavily in specific human capital. This leads to a lower wage.

2.2.1.1 Adjustment cost

In another contribution, Autor (2001) says that short-term work arrangements offer potential ways to avoid adjustment costs and as such represent an option value to the firm. Severance payments are nonexistent for short-term contracts. A firm's adjustment costs consist of hiring costs, firing costs and quit costs. The total costs are determined by the amount of turnover and the (hiring, firing and quit) costs per worker (Maurin, 2000).

Autor, (2000) states that the term of notice for employees influences quit costs. The shorter the employees' term of notice is, the higher is the probability that the firm experiences decreased productivity in the period between one worker quitting and the arrival of a new worker. This means that the implicit costs of quitting rise. Therefore, employers prefer longer terms of notice for their employees, so they can reduce the period of reduced productivity due to labour shortage.

Nevertheless, the period during which a firm experiences decreased productivity because one worker quits and another has not yet arrived can be considerably shorter if a replacement worker is provided. If an external party provides immediate replacement when an employee quits, quit and hiring costs decrease. This might be quite valuable to a firm, which accordingly is willing to pay for immediate replacement. The term of notice for employers is related to firing costs. The longer employers' term of notice, the higher the indirect costs of (reduced productivity during) dismissal procedures. So firing costs are higher, the longer the employers' term of notice is. Obviously, the same holds for the amount of severance payments, since these make up the direct cost element of firing costs. Not surprisingly, Autor, (2000) states that employers prefer shorter notice periods and lower severance payments and are willing to pay for that.

Kalleberg, (2000) reaffirms that lower firing costs are the reasons why these contracts are used, either for screening purposes or to absorb shocks in workload. As a result, it is unsurprising that fixed-term contracts are valued highest in industries that are sensitive to business cycle fluctuations such as manufacturing, for production, administrative and management personnel.

2.2.1.2 Training investments

The duration of stay of workers hired on short-term contracts is generally shorter than for regular workers, especially when used to absorb shocks. Therefore it is also unsurprising that several authors have found fewer training investments in short-term workers compared to regular workers (e.g. Bentolila and Bertola, 1990; Booth et al, 2002; Matindni, 2006); the payback period is shorter. When used for screening purposes, a fixed-term contract is usually explicitly contracted with the intensity to become permanent at the end of its term, if both parties are satisfied. In that case, expected duration is not so much shorter than for workers who work on an indefinite contract from the start, and thus it is not the reason for lower valuation and payment in that case. But screening is often the result of uncertainty about the worker's ability, which results in a risk deduction on the wage (Alvarez and Veracierto, 2005).

Houseman, (2001) contends that related trend to corporate downsizing has been outsourcing where companies contract with outside workers or agencies to perform non-core tasks. As a result, short-term contract agencies received some of the outsourcing business from these companies. Finally, increased regulation requiring employers to pay taxes on and provide various benefits to permanent employees also contributed to the demand for short-term contracts so that companies could bypass the additional measures or effort needed to comply with these regulations.

2.2.1.3Firing cost

While the objective of employment protection legislation is to reduce the exposure of employment relationships to unfair actions and to the risk of fluctuating incomes, these regulations may also increase the costs of hiring and firing workers. Firing regular employees with permanent work contracts may become very expensive due to high direct costs in form of severance payments as well as indirect costs that emerge from procedural difficulties (Bentolila and Bertola, 1990). From employers' point of view, it might be therefore cheaper to hire workers on the basis of short-term contracts, which have the advantage to reduce the firing costs because they end automatically after their expiry (Booth et al, 2002; Güell, 2003). The expected firing costs depend on the risk of dismissing the workers.

Güell, (2003) derive from his theoretical model that lower firing costs for short-term jobs reduces the likelihood that a short-term job will be converted into a permanent one. However, the empirical evidence so far shows that short-term contracts regulation has no effect on the incidences of short-term contracts controlling for the strictness of employment protection for regular workers (Booth et al., 2002; Kahn, 2005). Instead, the recent increase in the share of short-term contracts in some Western European countries has been explained by partial deregulation, i.e. the combination of high employment security for workers on permanent contracts and the removal of all hitherto barriers for the use of flexible short-term contracts (Riley, 2001).

The general argument of increased short-term work risk through strict regulations is only true in the case if wages cannot compensate for high firing costs (Autor, 2001). If there are no wage floors for permanent workers that prevent this kind of compensation, then firing costs need not raise the overall cost of offering permanent positions.

The mechanism of compensating the high firing costs with lower labour costs can be prevented by unions, which are the central labour market institution that affects wage setting. If unions compress wages by setting the floor at a high level (Alvarez et al., 2005), then collective bargaining may accentuate the effects of employment protection in shutting younger workers out of permanent jobs

2.2.2 Workload Fluctuation

Booth et al., (2000) states that short-term contracts are often regarded as an important component of achieving labour market flexibility; this is when the workload fluctuates. Short-term workers can be laid off without incurring statutory redundancy payments or restrictions imposed by employment rights legislation. It is also possible that firms maintain a high-turnover, low ability pool of short-term workers to adjust employment to match the existing workload. Individuals with low ability to acquire specific human capital will then go through a succession of low-paid, short-term jobs.

Using results from a research developed in six European countries and Israel, Nagypal (2001) suggests that companies hire short-term workers mainly for coping with flexibility needs (covering long absences, matching peaks on demands, covering short term absences and trial periods before offering permanent contracts) more than for long-term strategic motives such as saving costs or improving capabilities and performance. In this sense, employers will employ when the workload increases and shed some employees when the workload decreases. These fluctuations in activity may be short-term; hence employers do not see the need to keep employees for longer durations unnecessarily. It is therefore, a "hire when need arises" practice (Arai and Heyman, 2000).

Companies in educational sector were found to hire temporaries for filling vacancies and bringing specialized skills more than in industries and retail sector. Short-term workers preferred permanent contract, but in some cases, they reported advantages to accept a short-term arrangement. Companies from retail and industries use more frequently motives as matching peaks on demand, offering trial periods and covering unusual working hours than in education. Future prospects suggest than a third of companies expect workforce increases, and a half of them stay the same (Nagypal, 2001).

2.2.2.1 Covering Absences

Nagypal's (2001) findings are consistent with the findings of Booth et al (2000) who asserts that the main motives for hiring short-term employees are related with covering absences (both long term and short term), followed by offering trial periods before permanent contracts, and by matching staff to peaks in demands. These four motives were the most frequently used in most countries, but in different order.

Covering maternity and long term absences was the main motive reported by managers from the Netherlands, Belgium, UK and Spain, and the second motive in Sweden and Germany (Nagypal, 2000). Offering trial periods was the main motive reported by companies from Sweden and Israel and the third motive in The Netherlands and Spain. Matching staff with peaks in demands was reported as the main motive in Germany, and the second most important in The Netherlands, Spain, UK and Israel.

The reasons cited in a survey by Matindni, (2006) study for the use of flexible contracts are essentially cost, flexibility and fashion. Matindni found that short-term workers can provide greater flexibility because the number employed can vary to take account of changes in demand for the product or service; Short-term workers can also provide cover for permanent staff on holiday, maternity leave or sick leave; Short-term employees can provide specialist skills to carry out specific projects. Fixed term employment contracts have been introduced in a number of European countries as a way to provide flexibility to economies with high employment protection levels.

2.2.3 Business Uncertainty

It has been argued by Alvarez (2005) that companies use short-term workers because of the uncertainty about the future business trends. In a more specific argument, Arrow (1973) says that employers will use temporaries when they are unsure that the current positive business trends will continue in the foreseeable future or when they expect unfavorable business conditions. With the onset of the transition from socialism to market economies, employment rates dropped and unemployment increased substantially because the increased competition due to privatization and free markets led to downsizing the over-staffed public sector whereas the evolving new private sector was not able to absorb the labour resources of dismissed workers (Serrano, 1998; Kahn, 2005; Autor, 2001). As in Western Europe, rising unemployment and uncertainty through increased international competition and globalization called for labour market deregulation (Kahn, 2005).

However, short-term work has become a subject of fierce discussions in the scientific literature and in the public debate. On the one hand, proponents of labour market liberalization argue that short-term contracts provide a "bridge" to employment for jobseekers who, find particular difficulties in integration into the labour market, and additionally provide benefits for businesses by reducing firing costs and by increasing flexibility.

A contrasting perspective is that the short-term worker status is associated with lower wages, poor working conditions, and small chances for further promotion. For example, Arai and Heyman, (2000) interpret short-term contracts as a crucial new inequality because it erodes employment protection. Many empirical studies found evidence for this "segmentation" perspective in Western Europe (Kalleberg, 2000; Booth et al., 2002). Given disadvantages of short-term employment, the question becomes important who enters such employment relations.

2.2.4 Employee Screening

Some businesses use short-term contracts as a screening device for potential recruits to the permanent workforce (Houseman, 2001). Booth et al (2000) found evidence that short-term contracts are effective stepping-stones to permanent jobs. Firms may view the initial short-term contract as a probationary stage – subject to job performance and employment demand, workers will move into permanent employment at the firm. If the likelihood of eventual permanency is sufficiently high, the short-term job can be attractive to a worker of high ability even if it is low-paid. As argued by Loh, (1994) and by Wang and Weiss, (1998), cited in Booth et al. (2000), firms may seek to have the right workers self-select into probationary jobs by instituting a wide differential paid to the successful workers when they achieve permanency.

According to screening theory, employers may opt for short-term contracts as a form of prolonged probationary period that allows to better screen workers before employing them on a permanent basis (Arrow, 1973; Riley, 2001). Employers can be expected to recruit those applicants who can be considered to be both most productive and least costly for the kind of work required by the job.

However, information is incomplete in the labour market, i.e. job applicants' abilities are not completely observable for the employer and reveal only after the worker's performance on the job has been monitored for some time. Then, short-term contracts allow firms to obtain information that is unavailable before hiring an employee and that serves as a screening device for the quality of the match between worker and job. For those who fail to come up with the employers' expectations, the contract will not be converted into a permanent one ,Kalleberg (2000).

2.3 Concept of Short-term Contracting

Houseman, (2001) defines short-term contract as a contract which terminates on a specified date or on the occurrence of an event which is certain to occur on a particular date. On the other hand, Melchiomo, (1999) states that a short-term contract is normally used when no end date is known and its termination is dependent upon an event such as return from sick leave or maternity leave, or completion of a job.

Short-term contracts are characterized by the agreement between employer and employee on objective conditions under which a job ends, such as a specific date, the completion of a task or the return of another employee who has been temporarily replaced. In particular, this applies to occasional, casual or seasonal workers, short-term agency workers, workers on probationary period as well as workers with a contract for a specific task (Amuedo-Dorantes, 2001).

The same view is supported by Kalleberg, (2000) who affirms that short-term employees typically work for firms for brief and often fixed periods, in contrast with permanent full- and part-time workers. Companies typically use short-term help for employee absences, special assignments, seasonal work increases, and short-term worker shortages (Houseman, 2001).

Abowd et al, (1999) poses that employees on fixed term contracts have the right to be paid the same rate as similar permanent employees working for the same employer and in general terms should not be treated less favorably than permanent employees. This means that employees on fixed term contracts will have broadly the same rights to statutory redundancy payments, written reasons for dismissal and the right not to be unfairly dismissed as permanent employees.

2.4 Review of Past Studies

A confluence of factors fueled the growth of short-term contracts including corporate downsizing or restructuring, low unemployment rates, outsourcing, and increased employment regulation. Downsizing refers to the corporation practice of reducing the size of their core workforce. Houseman, (2001) says that short-term employees provide firms with a great deal of flexibility in the face of changing business conditions. The trend of substitution of short-term for permanent workers is reflected in the fact that the decline in short-term contracts was substantially less in the recession of the early 1980s than in the recessions of the 1970s (Houseman, 2001).

In his 1988 volume, Alternative Staffing Strategies, Nye, (cited in Autor, 2001) argued that the expanded use of short-term contracts was likely to persist. He wrote that factors that caused the growth of short-term contracts are expected to continue exerting an influence on the labor market. According to Nye, these factors include the decline of manufacturing jobs and the growth information, technology, and service jobs, employer reliance on short-term contracts to help cope with possible business slowdowns, the growth of technology that requires specialization, and the presence workers with adequate skills who by choice or out of necessity seek short-term employment.

More than 95% of all businesses studied by Nye, (1988) used short-term staffing as a management strategy to balance workforce needs year round. Whether it is as a solution to employee absences, a coping mechanism for varying work cycles or simply as a means to launch a special project, the flexible, contingent workforce had become an integral part of corporate America.

Companies are increasingly recognizing the usefulness of short-term staff for an adaptable workforce to help them increase efficiency, cope with new technologies and deal with customer demand, seasonal fluctuations and economic uncertainty. The companies also do not need to provide benefits and holiday pay to the short-term workers and do not need to burden permanent employees with more work if it is needed (Güell and Petrongolo, 2003).

In a 2002 study, Booth et al found that in Britain about 7% of male employees and 10% of female employees were in short-term jobs. In contrast to much of continental Europe, this proportion was found to have been relatively stable over the 1990s. Using data from the British Household Panel Survey, Booth et al found that short-term workers reported lower levels of job satisfaction, received less work-related training, and were less well-paid than their counterparts in permanent employment. However, there was evidence that fixed-term contracts were a stepping stone to permanent work. Women (but not men) who started in fixed-term employment and moved to permanent jobs fully caught up to those who started in permanent jobs.

Autor, (2001) asserts that it is generally acknowledged that short-term and flexible types of employment have been created to escape from stringent employment regulation. Once the probation period has passed it is hard to dismiss workers on indefinite contracts in many countries. Fixed-term contracts are often used as extended probationary periods, after which employees who perform on a satisfactory level are offered an indefinite contract. Also, fixed-term contracts are used for activities that are known in advance to last only for a certain period of time. The following sections review past studies regarding increased use of short-term contracts.

2.5 Critical Review

Short-term work has become a subject of fierce discussions in the scientific literature and in the public debate. On the one hand, proponents of labour market flexibility argue that short-term contracts provide a "bridge" to employment for jobseekers who, find particular difficulties in integration into the labour market, and additionally provide benefits for businesses by reducing firing costs and by increasing flexibility. A contrasting perspective is that the short-term worker status is associated with lower wages, poor working conditions, and small chances for further promotion. Furthermore, a particular shortcoming of the literature about short-term contracts is that it has largely disregarded employers' perspective.

2.6 Summary

The factors that motivated firms to employ workers on short-term basis had not been exhaustively investigated. This study added another variable- business uncertainty which appeared in the literature but was not investigated by the researchers. This study investigates why short-term contracts practice is favoured /desire by firms to cut costs; employee screening before being awarded permanent contracts; uncertainty about the future of the business; and the desire to achieve labour flexibility.

The study was conducted from the employers' perspective and not the employee's perspective as had been done by researchers before such as (Houseman, 2001; Booth et al, 2000).

CHAPTER THREE

3.0 RESEARCH DESIGN AND METHODOLOGY

3.1 Introduction

This chapter sets out the research methodology adopted so as to meet the objectives stated in chapter one of this study to work around the problem of the study. It also spells out the research setting, the populations of interest, the sample, data collection instruments, and data analysis techniques that was used .

3.2 Research Design

This study adopted a descriptive survey design. The core advantage of descriptive design is that it seeks to establish factors associated with certain occurrences, outcomes, conditions or types of behavior(Mugenda & Mugenda 2001) .This method was preferred because it allowed an in-depth study of the subject matter. The other advantage was that descriptive studies make use of questionnaires with which is easier to collect and analyze data.

3.3 Population

The target population of the study entails the commercial banks in Kenya. The study covers 45 registered commercial banks in Kenya (CBK, 2009). This is because these banks as indicated in the past have a recorded high statistics of human resource procurement through this method and hence it is expected to yield more informed information about the factor favouring increased use of this form of contracting. Moreover, all the commercial banks have their head quarters in Nairobi which is the capital city of Kenya, it is expected to host many jobless seekers who may be the subject of this form of contracting.

23

3.4 Sampling Frame

The sampling Frame constituted a list of commercial banks obtained from Central Bank of Kenya. Then for data collection, structured questionnaires were targeted to be distributed to the human resource managers of the banking institutions as the respondents. The data collected was assumed to take care of both primary and secondary information.

3.5 The Sampling Technique

The study employed a census of the entire 45 registered commercial banks in Kenya, based in Nairobi city. Since information on Human Resource Procurement is available in Human Resource Department, the Human resource manager was the respondent. The Human Resource department was the unit under observation. A purposive kind of sampling where the structured questionnaires were handed to the human resources officers of each of the registered commercial bank. A complete enumeration of the listed commercial banks was used for collection of data to meet the research objectives.

3.6 Data Description and Collection

The study collected both primary and secondary data. The primary data was collected through a semi structured questionnaire which was interviewer administered. This ensured accuracy of the information obtained which is expected to lessen the errors. On the other hand, secondary data was collected through a thorough review of both the empirical and theoretical literatures in this field of human resource and procurement and the scenarios and profiles of the banking business in Kenya.

3.7 Pilot testing

Pre-testing was carried out to ensure that the items in the instrument were stated clear and had the same meaning to all respondents. The respondents on which the instrument was pre-tested should were not part of the selected sample. Pre-testing assessed the clarity and ease of use of the instrument. The researcher was also able to assess the time taken to administer the instrument. Items that confused the respondents were modified. Information obtained during pre-testing was used to revise the instrument. Data obtained was analyzed and results used to develop dummy tables.

3.8 Data Analysis and Presentation

The study was expected to generate qualitative data. The data was coded, cleaned and checked for completeness. Simple descriptive statistics will be generated using the SPSS (Statistical Package for Social Sciences) which is a computerized statistical environment. The qualitative data will be analyzed by describing, structuring, categorizing, and combining into relevant themes. The data will then be presented using frequency tables of percentage counts and various figures.

CHAPTER FOUR

4.0 DATA ANALYSIS PRESENTATION AND INTERPRETATION

4.1 Introduction

This chapter presents the data that was obtained from 45 institutions that successfully responded for the study. The data was analyzed in percentages and illustrated by the use of tables and figures for visual comparison.

4.2 Characteristics of Organizations Studied

4.2.1 Response Rate

Fourty five banks were targeted for the study and out of these, thirty nine banks gave a full response to the questionnaires of the study. This constitutes an overwhelming (86.7%) response rate which is considered adequate for this study. in fact, most of the researcher and scholars consider (70%) response rate as adequate for descriptive research. This presented in the following table 4.1.

Table 4.1: Response Rate

Responses	Percentage (%)
Responded	86.7
Not Responded	13.3
Total	**100**

4.2.2 Age of the Firms

The question sought to establish the number of years the organizations had been in existence. Most (36.4%) of the organizations were existing between 20 to 30 years; 27.2% were more than 30 years old; 18.2% percent were aged between 10 to 20 years; and another 18.2% had been in existence for less than 10 years. This information is important because the number of years which these banks existed can give further insights on their experiences to establish the labour trends and take appropriate decisions. This information is depicted in the table 4.2 below.

Table 4.2: Age of the Firms

Responses	Percentage (%)
Below 10 years	18.2
10 to 20 years	18.2
20 to 30 years	36.4
Above 30 years	27.2
Total	**100**

4.2.3 Level of Short-term Employment

The question was set to determine the percentage of employees that were employed on short-term contracts. Majority (54.6.%) said they had between five percent and ten percent of their employees on short-term contracts while 27.2% of the firms surveyed reported a staff proportion of less than 5% on short-term contracts. This shows that the percentage of employees on short-term contracts were between 5% and 10%. The results are indicated in figure 4.1 in the next page.

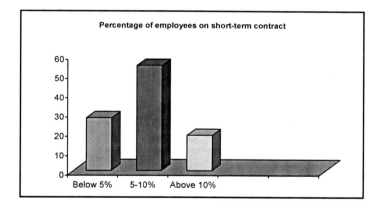

Figure 4.1: Employees on Short-Term Contracts

4.2.4 Types of Short-Term Workers

27

This question sought to investigate the types of short-term workers that were hired by the organizations. Majority (65%) indicated that they hired on-call workers, 23% indicated that they hired fixed-term workers. while casual employees were hired by a paltry 12% of the firms surveyed none hired freelance. This is as shown in figure 4.2. This indicates that on-call workers are the employees mostly hired on temporary basis. This therefore suggests that the fluctuation in work demands is not predictable and hence addressed according to the need.

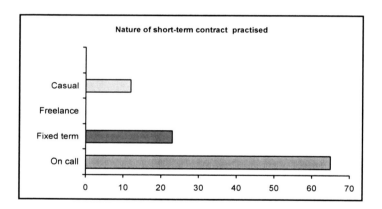

Figure 4.2: Nature of Short-term contract practiced

4.3 Cost Implication of Short- Term Contracts

4.3.1 Short Term Employment Savings on Wage Costs

The question was sought to establish whether the banks' practice of short-term employment saved on wage costs. Majority, (90.9%) of the respondents felt that the practice saves on wage cost while a paltry

28

(9.1%) of the respondents felt otherwise as shown in table 4.2. short term contracting is an organizations human resource strategy which must be aligned with other business strategies. This is therefore expected since the main objective is to save cost and increase profit.

Table 4.3: Whether Short Term Employment Savings on Wage Costs

Responses	Percentage (%)
Saves	90.9
Don't save	9.1
Total	**100**

4.3.2 Short Term Employment Savings on Training Costs

The question was meant to establish whether short term contract saves on the cost incurred by the organization on training. Majority, (63.6%) thought the contract it doesn't saves training cost while the rest (36.4%) believe this can saves on the training expenses. This is expected since it is for short terms only but other full time employees are still required to go for various training to up grade their skills. It is not a wonder such contracting is even necessary when other employees go for training.

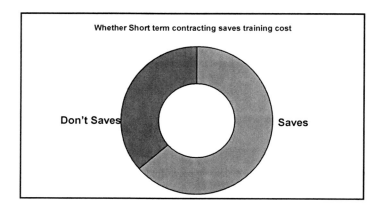

Whether Short term contracting saves training cost

Don't Saves   Saves

Figure 4.3 whether short term contracting saves training cost

4.3.3 Short Term Employment Savings on Fringe-Benefit Costs

Respondents were also asked to indicate whether short-term employment saves on fringe-benefit costs. Majority, (81.8%) of the respondents agreed that it saves on the cost on fringe benefits while (18.2%) felt that short-term employment saved on fringe-benefit costs. This shows that short term employment saved on employee fringe-benefit costs incurred by the organizations since employees contracted on such terms automatically don't qualify for this benefit.

30

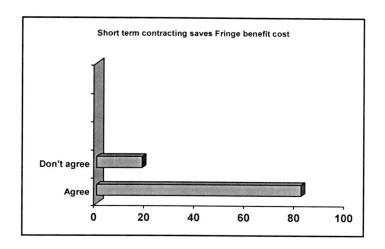

Figure 4.4: Short Term Employment Saves on Fringe-Benefit Costs

4.4 Workload Fluctuation and Short-Term Contracts

4.4.1 Offsetting High Workload Demands

This question sought to investigate whether the respondents use the short term contracting as a strategy to off set high workloads during peak sessions. All (100%) confided that the main reason for this form of contracting is mainly to reduce the staff workload and give them a helping hand. This finding is important since the overwhelming response underscores the significance of the short term contracting in the banking sector. Indeed there are some peak seasons when the number of transaction or the customers seeking banking services is higher which require this intervention.

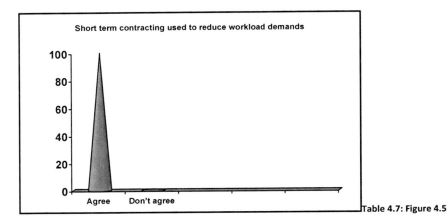

Short-Term Contracts used to reduce Workload Demands

4.4.2 Short-Term Contracts and Short-Term Employee Absence

The question was meant to find out if firms used short-term employment so as to cover up for periods when staff was on short term absence. Majority (81.8%) of the respondents agreed that it is used to cover short term employee absence while 18.2% said did not agree this reason. This is presented in the following table 4.4. Nevertheless, this findings is in agreement with the previous analysis and perhaps the banks as business organizations seems to be having difficulties in predicting and forecasting the its human resource requirements strategically and proactively.

Table 4.4: Whether employee short term absence prompted short term contracting

Responses	Percentage (%)
Agree	81.8

Disagree	18.2
Total	**100**

4.4.3 Short-Term Contracts and Long-Term Employee Absence

This question sought to establish whether firms used short term contracts so as to cover for longer
periods of staff absence. Majority (77%) of the respondents said agreed the contracting as a measure for
covering the long term employee absence while the rest (23%) felt otherwise. This is still in agreement
with the previous case of short term employee absence. Perhaps the factor 'absence' regardless of
whether it is long or short term will still requires this contracting decision.

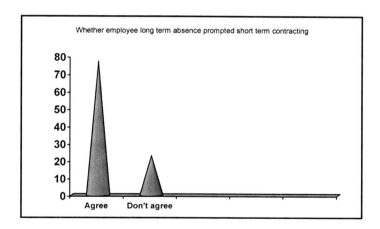

Figure 4.6: Whether employee long term absence prompted short term contracting

4.5 Business Uncertainty and Short-Term Contracting

4.5.1 Short term contracting as a Precautionary Measure

The question required from respondents whether they used short-term contracts so as to bring in special skills for precautionary measures. Majority (91.0%) said thought this is a strategic activity that helps in combating business uncertainties while a paltry (9.0%) felt otherwise. This is reflected in the table 4.5. It is therefore not a wonder when the business landscape is continuously becoming unpredictable due to ever increasing competitiveness.

Table 4.5: Short term contracting as a Precautionary Measure

Responses	Percentage (%)
Used as a precautions	91
Not used as a precautions	9
Total	**100**

4.5.2 Whether Firms Use Short Term to have Personnel for Unusual Working Hours

This question sought to investigate whether respondents used short term contracts to have personnel for unusual working hours. An overwhelming majority (90.9%) disagreed to this idea while 9.1% agreed as shown in figure 4.7. This is an indication \that firms intention to contract employee on short term basis is not for exploiting during unusual odd hours or session. This could perhaps be due to the security reasons which may not trust the work with the part timers at unusual hours.

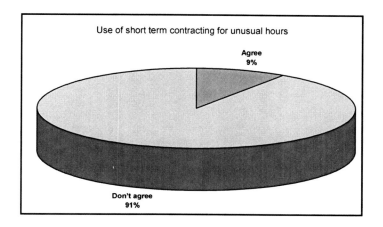

Figure 4.7: Use of short term contracting for unusual hours

4.6 Employee Screening and Short-Term Contracting

4.6.1 Use of Short Term Contracts for Probationary Periods

This question sought to investigate whether contracting employees on short term basis is a way of putting employees under probation. An overwhelming majority (76%) of the respondents did agree that they use short term contracting as a strategy to put their newly contracted employees on probation. 24% disagreed. This may indicated that banks use short term contracting to put their employees on probation so that they have the discretion to renew or terminate the contract. The following table shows the findings.

35

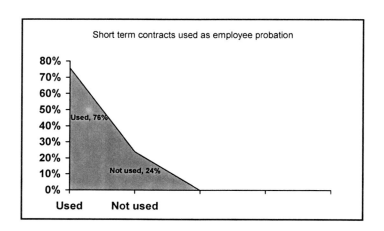

Figure 4.8: Short term contracts used as employee probation

4.6.2 Short Term Contracts used as transition to permanent contracts

The purpose of this question was to determine whether organizations used short term contracts as transition to permanent contracts for their employees. An overwhelming majority (81.8%) of the respondents said yes while 18.2% said no. This indicates that most banks used this contracting as a form of transition to permanent contracts for employees. This is shown in figure 4.9. This could perhaps be a growing trend of cutting cost through this form of procurement than advertising and going through a laborious task of recruitment and selection.

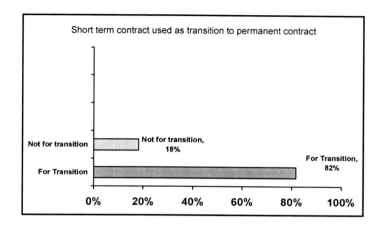

Figure 4.9: Short Term Contracts used as transition to permanent contracts

4.6.3 Effectiveness of Short term Contracts

The question sought to establish whether short term contracts was an effective way to screen employees for more permanent jobs for the surveyed firms. Most (72.7%) of the respondents felt this form of contracting as effective while (27.3%) felt not. This is in agreement with the entire finding that has been displaying position opinion for the use of this form of human resource procurement in the banking sector.

Table 4.6: Opinion on the Perceived Effectiveness of Short term Contracting

Responses	Percentage
Yes	72.7

No	27.3
Total	100

CHAPTER FIVE

5.0   SUMMARY, CONCLUSIONS AND RECOMMENDATIONS

5.1 Introduction

This chapter presents a summary of the findings, conclusions, and recommendations of the study based on the specific objectives that guided the entire research. It comprises of the summary of the major findings, conclusions and recommendations.

5.2 Summary of the Major Findings

5.2.1 Cost Implication of Short- Term Employment

The study found that the cost implication of short-term contracts is less severe than permanent employment contracts. Out of the firms surveyed 91% indicated that short-term contracts save d on their wage costs, while 82% indicated that it saved on fringe-benefit costs paid to employees with the same proportion saying that short term employment saved on firing costs. However, 64% did not think that short-term employment helped them save on training costs.

5.2.2 Workload Fluctuation

The study found that 100% of the firms employed people on short-term basis so as to match staff to peak workload demands, 82% used short-term contracts to cover short-term absence of permanent staff while 73% indicated that they use short-term employment to cover longer periods of staff absences.

5.2.3 Business Uncertainty

The firms surveyed used short-term employment as precaution for some form of business uncertainty with 91% indicating that they used short-term employment to have personnel for unusual working hours and another 64% saying that they used short-term employment because their organizations were uncertain about future business. However less than (45%) said they increasingly used short-term contracts to to freeze on permanent employee numbers while 36% said they wanted to bring in special skills for precautionary measures.

5.2.4 Employee Screening Practices

73% of the firms surveyed used short term employment contracts for employee probationary periods, 82% used use short term contracts as transition to permanent contracts for employees while another 73% indicated that short term contract was an effective way to screen employees for more permanent jobs.

5.3 Conclusions

The study concludes that the factors that contribute to increased use of short-term employments contracts is because these contracts are effective in saving costs; they can b used to match staff numbers to workload fluctuation ; they are suitable when there is business uncertainty; and that they provide a criteria to screen employees on the on the job.

As indicated in the findings, short-term contracts were found to save wage costs, fringe-benefits and costs of firing employees for most of the firms. The study also concludes that fluctuating workload can fuel increased use of short-term contract as businesses seek to match staff to peak workload demands or to cover up for long and short-term absence of permanent staff. Furthermore, business uncertainty has caused most of the firms to employ on short-term basis because they needed staff to for unusual work hours or because the future of the firm was uncertain.

It was indicated by 73% of the firms that short-term employment was an effective way to screen employees for more permanent jobs. To this extend short-term employment was used by the firms as transition to permanent contracts for employees. From the study the main motives for hiring employees on short-term basis were related with matching staff to peak workload demands, saving on wage costs, having personnel for unusual working hours, covering staff absences (both long term and short term), and screening employees before giving them permanent jobs.

5.4 Recommendations

The study suggest that companies can hire temporary workers mainly for coping with flexibility needs such as covering long absences, matching peaks on demands and trial periods before offering permanent contracts. The short-term contracts also provide cost saving benefits in paying wages, allowances and benefits to employees. However, firms should employ on short-term basis with caution because of the job insecurity that this arrangement signal to the employees. In this regard they may feel de-motivated and spend most of their time searching for the next job.

Area for Further Research

This study could be a rung in the ladder to deeper studies that include more samples of forms. It would be of great significance to categorize the various motives of using temporary employment contracts by firms of different industries. Another dimension would be to study the short-term workers themselves to understand why they accept the short-term employment arrangement. This study could be conducted among all temporary employees with different types of contracts (fixed-term, daily/on call, on probation, training, seasonal, contractors, etc.).

REFERENCES

Abowd, J. Corbel, P. and Kramarz, F. (1999). *The Entry and Exit of Workers and the Growth of Employment: An analysis of French Establishments.* Review of Economics and Statistics 81, 170-187.

Adam, P, Canziani, P (1998).*Partial deregulation: fixed-term contracts in Italy and Spain.* Center for Economic Performance, discussion paper.

Alvarez, F and Veracierto, M., (2005). *Fixed-Term Employment Contracts in an Equilibrium Search Model.* Federal Reserve Bank of Chicago, Working Paper No.14. Available at SSRN: http://ssrn.com/abstract=869437

Amuedo-Dorantes, C. (2001) .*From short-term to permanent, promoting permanent employment in Spain,* International Journal of Manpower, Vol. 22 No.7, pp.625-47.

Arai, M. and Heyman, F. (2000). *Permanent and Short-term Labor*: Gross Job and Worker Flows in Sweden, 1989-98, Working Paper, no. 71, National Institute of Economic Research, Stockholm.

Autor, D. H (2001). *Why Do Short-term Help Firms Provide Free General Skills Training?.* The Quarterly Journal of Economics, MIT Press, vol. 116(4), pages 1409-1448, November.

Bentolila, S. and Bertola, G. (1990). *Firing Costs and Labour Demand: How Bad is Eurosclerosis?.* The Review of Economic Studies 57(3), 381-402.

Booth, A. L et al, 2002. *Short-term Jobs: Stepping Stones Or Dead Ends?.* Economic Journal, Royal Economic Society, vol. 112(480), pages F189-F213, June. Available at ftp://repec.iza.org/RePEc/Discussionpaper/dp205.pdf

Güell, M., and Petrongolo, B. (2003), *Workers transitions from short-term to permanent employment: the Spanish case,* Discussion Paper 438, CEP.

Houseman, S N. (2001).*Why Employers Use Flexible Staffing Arrangements: Evidence from an Employer Survey.* Industrial and Labor Relations Review 55(1): 149–170.

Hunt, J, 2000. *Firing Costs, Employment Fluctuations and Average Employment: An Examination of Germany,* Economica. London School of Economics and Political Science, vol. 67(266), pages 177-202, May.

Kahn, L. (2005). *The Impact of Employment Protection Mandates on Demographic Short-term contracts Patterns: International Microeconomic Evidence.* Discussion Paper No. 1548. IZA, Cologne.

Kalleberg, A. (2000). *Nonstandard Employment Relations; Part-Time, Short-term and Contract Work.* Annual Review of Sociology 26, 341-65.

Matindni, K (2006). *An insight into short-term contracts practice: A survey of companies in Kenya;* MBA thesis (Unpublished).

Nagypal, E (2001). *Fixed-term Contracts in Europe: A Reassessment.* Stanford , University manuscript.

Riley, J. (2001). *Silver Signals: Twenty-Five Years of Screening and Signaling.* Journal Of Economic Literature 39, 432-78.

APPENDIX 1

QUESTIONNAIRE

The purpose of this questionnaire is to gather information on the factors favouring increased use of short-term contracts within the Kenyan Banking Industry. The information obtained from the respondents shall be treated with strict confidentiality and shall only be used for the purpose of this academic research. Your participation shall be highly appreciated.

SECTION I

PART A: GENERAL INFORMATION

1) Name of the organisation (optional)_____

2) Number of years the organization has been in existence

      ☐ Below 10 years

      ☐ 10-20 years

      ☐ 20-30 years

      ☐ Above 30 years

3) What is the approximate percentage of the total number of your employees that are on short-term contracts?

☐ Below 5%

☐ 5-10%

☐ Above 10%

4)   What kind of employees do you employ on short-term contracts on a regular basis?

☐ Casual employees (called upon on day-basis)

☐ On-call workers

☐ Fixed-term workers (employment on fixed duration)

☐ Freelance workers/ contractors

☐ Other _____

SECTION II

The questions from Part A to Part E are aimed at gathering information on your reasons for using short-term contracts. Please tick all that apply.

PART B: COST IMPLICATION OF SHORT- TERM EMPLOYMENT

5)   Short-term contracts save on the wage costs

Agree ☐   Disagree ☐

6)   Short-term contracts save on the training costs

Agree ☐   Disagree ☐

7)   Short-term contracts save on fringe-benefit costs

          Agree ☐   Disagree ☐

8)   Short-term contracts save on firing costs

          Agree ☐   Disagree ☐

PART C: WORKLOAD FLUCTUATION

Do you use short-term contracts

9)   To match staff to peak workload demands

          Yes ☐   No ☐

10)   To cover staff short-term absence

          Yes ☐   No ☐

11)   To cover long periods of staff absences

          Yes ☐   No ☐

PART D: BUSINESS UNCERTAINTY

Do you use short-term contracts

12)   To bring in special skills for precautionary measures

Yes ☐   No ☐

13)   To have personnel for unusual working hours

Yes ☐   No ☐

14)   Because we need to freeze on permanent employee numbers

Yes ☐   No ☐

15)   Because the organization is uncertain about its future business

Yes ☐   No ☐

PART E: EMPLOYEE SCREENING PRACTICES

16)   Do you use short-term employment contracts for employee probationary periods

Yes ☐   No ☐

17)   Do you use short-term contracts as transition to permanent contracts for employees

Yes ☐   No ☐

18)   Are Short-term contract an effective way to screen employees for more permanent jobs

Yes ☐   No ☐

CPSIA information can be obtained at www.ICGtesting.com
Printed in the USA
LVOW081807240213

321460LV00002B/413/P